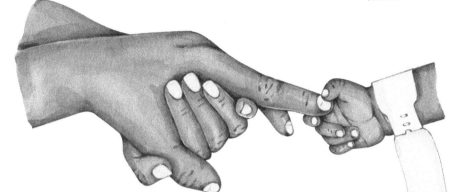

BABY SHOWER

In Celebration of

_____

_____

_____

Date

_____

Baby Shower

Name: ....

Relationship to the parents / baby: ....

Wishes for the parents: ....

....

....

Wishes for the baby: ....

....

....

My best advice for parents: ....

....

....

Baby Shower

Name: ....

Relationship to the parents / baby: ....

Wishes for the parents: ....

....

....

Wishes for the baby: ....

....

....

My best advice for parents: ....

....

....

♡ Baby Shower ♡

Name: ....

Relationship to the parents / baby: ....

Wishes for the parents: ....

....

....

Wishes for the baby: ....

....

....

My best advice for parents: ....

....

....

Baby Shower

Name: ....

Relationship to the parents / baby: ....

Wishes for the parents: ....

....

....

Wishes for the baby: ....

....

....

My best advice for parents: ....

....

....

Baby Shower

Name: ....

Relationship to the parents / baby: ....

Wishes for the parents: ....

....

....

Wishes for the baby: ....

....

....

My best advice for parents: ....

....

....

♡ Baby Shower ♡

Name: ....

Relationship to the parents / baby: ....

Wishes for the parents: ....

....

....

Wishes for the baby: ....

....

....

My best advice for parents: ....

....

....

Baby Shower

Name: ....

Relationship to the parents / baby: ....

Wishes for the parents: ....

....

....

Wishes for the baby: ....

....

....

My best advice for parents: ....

....

....

♡ Baby Shower ♡

Name: ....

Relationship to the parents / baby: ....

Wishes for the parents: ....

....

....

Wishes for the baby: ....

....

....

My best advice for parents: ....

....

....

Baby Shower

Name: ....

Relationship to the parents / baby: ....

Wishes for the parents: ....

....

....

Wishes for the baby: ....

....

....

My best advice for parents: ....

....

....

♡ Baby Shower ♡

Name: ....

Relationship to the parents / baby: ....

Wishes for the parents: ....

....

....

Wishes for the baby: ....

....

....

My best advice for parents: ....

....

....

Baby Shower

Name: ....

Relationship to the parents / baby: ....

Wishes for the parents: ....

....

....

Wishes for the baby: ....

....

....

My best advice for parents: ....

....

....

Baby Shower

Name: ....

Relationship to the parents / baby: ....

Wishes for the parents: ....

....

....

Wishes for the baby: ....

....

....

My best advice for parents: ....

....

....

Baby Shower

Name: ....

Relationship to the parents / baby: ....

Wishes for the parents: ....

....

....

Wishes for the baby: ....

....

....

My best advice for parents: ....

....

....

Baby Shower

Name: ....

Relationship to the parents / baby: ....

Wishes for the parents: ....

....

....

Wishes for the baby: ....

....

....

My best advice for parents: ....

....

....

Baby Shower

Name: ....

Relationship to the parents / baby: ....

Wishes for the parents: ....

....

....

Wishes for the baby: ....

....

....

My best advice for parents: ....

....

....

♡ Baby Shower ♡

Name: ....

Relationship to the parents / baby: ....

Wishes for the parents: ....

....

....

Wishes for the baby: ....

....

....

My best advice for parents: ....

....

....

Baby Shower

Name: ....

Relationship to the parents / baby: ....

Wishes for the parents: ....

....

....

Wishes for the baby: ....

....

....

My best advice for parents: ....

....

....

Baby Shower

Name: ....

Relationship to the parents / baby: ....

Wishes for the parents: ....

....

....

Wishes for the baby: ....

....

....

My best advice for parents: ....

....

....

Baby Shower

Name: ....

Relationship to the parents / baby: ....

Wishes for the parents: ....

....

....

Wishes for the baby: ....

....

....

My best advice for parents: ....

....

....

Baby Shower

Name: ....

Relationship to the parents / baby: ....

Wishes for the parents: ....

....

....

Wishes for the baby: ....

....

....

My best advice for parents: ....

....

....

Baby Shower

Name: ....

Relationship to the parents / baby: ....

Wishes for the parents: ....
....
....

Wishes for the baby: ....
....
....

My best advice for parents: ....
....
....

♡ Baby Shower ♡

Name: ....

Relationship to the parents / baby: ....

Wishes for the parents: ....

....

....

Wishes for the baby: ....

....

....

My best advice for parents: ....

....

....

Baby Shower

Name: ....

Relationship to the parents / baby: ....

Wishes for the parents: ....

....

....

Wishes for the baby: ....

....

....

My best advice for parents: ....

....

....

Baby Shower

Name: ....

Relationship to the parents / baby: ....

Wishes for the parents: ....

....

....

Wishes for the baby: ....

....

....

My best advice for parents: ....

....

....

Baby Shower

Name: ....

Relationship to the parents / baby: ....

Wishes for the parents: ....

....

....

Wishes for the baby: ....

....

....

My best advice for parents: ....

....

....

♡ Baby Shower ♡

Name: ....

Relationship to the parents / baby: ....

Wishes for the parents: ....

....

....

Wishes for the baby: ....

....

....

My best advice for parents: ....

....

....

Baby Shower

Name: ....

Relationship to the parents / baby: ....

Wishes for the parents: ....

....

....

Wishes for the baby: ....

....

....

My best advice for parents: ....

....

....

♡ Baby Shower ♡

Name: ....

Relationship to the parents / baby: ....

Wishes for the parents: ....

....

....

Wishes for the baby: ....

....

....

My best advice for parents: ....

....

....

♡ Baby Shower ♡

Name: ....

Relationship to the parents / baby: ....

Wishes for the parents: ....

....

....

Wishes for the baby: ....

....

....

My best advice for parents: ....

....

....

Baby Shower

Name: ....

Relationship to the parents / baby: ....

Wishes for the parents: ....

....

....

Wishes for the baby: ....

....

....

My best advice for parents: ....

....

....

Baby Shower

Name: ....

Relationship to the parents / baby: ....

Wishes for the parents: ....

....

....

Wishes for the baby: ....

....

....

My best advice for parents: ....

....

....

Baby Shower

Name: ....

Relationship to the parents / baby: ....

Wishes for the parents: ....

....

....

Wishes for the baby: ....

....

....

My best advice for parents: ....

....

....

Baby Shower

Name: ....

Relationship to the parents / baby: ....

Wishes for the parents: ....

....

....

Wishes for the baby: ....

....

....

My best advice for parents: ....

....

....

♡ Baby Shower ♡

Name: ....

Relationship to the parents / baby: ....

Wishes for the parents: ....

....

....

Wishes for the baby: ....

....

....

My best advice for parents: ....

....

....

♡ Baby Shower ♡

Name: ....

Relationship to the parents / baby: ....

Wishes for the parents: ....

....

....

Wishes for the baby: ....

....

....

My best advice for parents: ....

....

....

Baby Shower

Name: ....

Relationship to the parents / baby: ....

Wishes for the parents: ....

....

....

Wishes for the baby: ....

....

....

My best advice for parents: ....

....

....

♡ Baby Shower ♡

Name: ....

Relationship to the parents / baby: ....

Wishes for the parents: ....

....

....

Wishes for the baby: ....

....

....

My best advice for parents: ....

....

....

♡ Baby Shower ♡

Name: ....

Relationship to the parents / baby: ....

Wishes for the parents: ....

....

....

Wishes for the baby: ....

....

....

My best advice for parents: ....

....

....

Baby Shower

Name: ....

Relationship to the parents / baby: ....

Wishes for the parents: ....

....

....

Wishes for the baby: ....

....

....

My best advice for parents: ....

....

....

Baby Shower

Name: ....

Relationship to the parents / baby: ....

Wishes for the parents: ....

....

....

Wishes for the baby: ....

....

....

My best advice for parents: ....

....

....

Baby Shower

Name: ....

Relationship to the parents / baby: ....

Wishes for the parents: ....

....

....

Wishes for the baby: ....

....

....

My best advice for parents: ....

....

....

Baby Shower

Name: ....

Relationship to the parents / baby: ....

Wishes for the parents: ....

....

....

Wishes for the baby: ....

....

....

My best advice for parents: ....

....

....

Baby Shower

Name: ....

Relationship to the parents / baby: ....

Wishes for the parents: ....

....

....

Wishes for the baby: ....

....

....

My best advice for parents: ....

....

....

♡ Baby Shower ♡

Name: ....

Relationship to the parents / baby: ....

Wishes for the parents: ....

....

....

Wishes for the baby: ....

....

....

My best advice for parents: ....

....

....

♡ Baby Shower ♡

Name: ....

Relationship to the parents / baby: ....

Wishes for the parents: ....

....

....

Wishes for the baby: ....

....

....

My best advice for parents: ....

....

....

Baby Shower

Name: ....

Relationship to the parents / baby: ....

Wishes for the parents: ....

....

....

Wishes for the baby: ....

....

....

My best advice for parents: ....

....

....

♡ Baby Shower ♡

Name: ....

Relationship to the parents / baby: ....

Wishes for the parents: ....

....

....

Wishes for the baby: ....

....

....

My best advice for parents: ....

....

....

Baby Shower

Name: ....

Relationship to the parents / baby: ....

Wishes for the parents: ....

....

....

Wishes for the baby: ....

....

....

My best advice for parents: ....

....

....

Baby Shower

Name: ....

Relationship to the parents / baby: ....

Wishes for the parents: ....

....

....

Wishes for the baby: ....

....

....

My best advice for parents: ....

....

....

Baby Shower

Name: ....

Relationship to the parents / baby: ....

Wishes for the parents: ....

....

....

Wishes for the baby: ....

....

....

My best advice for parents: ....

....

....

♡ Baby Shower ♡

Name: ....

Relationship to the parents / baby: ....

Wishes for the parents: ....

....

....

Wishes for the baby: ....

....

....

My best advice for parents: ....

....

....

Baby Shower

Name: ....

Relationship to the parents / baby: ....

Wishes for the parents: ....

....

....

Wishes for the baby: ....

....

....

My best advice for parents: ....

....

....

Baby Shower

Name: ....

Relationship to the parents / baby: ....

Wishes for the parents: ....

....

....

Wishes for the baby: ....

....

....

My best advice for parents: ....

....

....

♡ Baby Shower ♡

Name: ....

Relationship to the parents / baby: ....

Wishes for the parents: ....

....

....

Wishes for the baby: ....

....

....

My best advice for parents: ....

....

....

Baby Shower

Name: ....

Relationship to the parents / baby: ....

Wishes for the parents: ....
....
....

Wishes for the baby: ....
....
....

My best advice for parents: ....
....
....

♡ Baby Shower ♡

Name: ....

Relationship to the parents / baby: ....

Wishes for the parents: ....

....

....

Wishes for the baby: ....

....

....

My best advice for parents: ....

....

....

Baby Shower

Name: ....

Relationship to the parents / baby: ....

Wishes for the parents: ....

....

....

Wishes for the baby: ....

....

....

My best advice for parents: ....

....

....

Baby Shower

Name: ....

Relationship to the parents / baby: ....

Wishes for the parents: ....

....

....

Wishes for the baby: ....

....

....

My best advice for parents: ....

....

....

♡ Baby Shower ♡

Name: ....

Relationship to the parents / baby: ....

Wishes for the parents: ....

....

....

Wishes for the baby: ....

....

....

My best advice for parents: ....

....

....

Baby Shower

Name: ....

Relationship to the parents / baby: ....

Wishes for the parents: ....

....

....

Wishes for the baby: ....

....

....

My best advice for parents: ....

....

....

♡ Baby Shower ♡

Name: ....

Relationship to the parents / baby: ....

Wishes for the parents: ....

....

....

Wishes for the baby: ....

....

....

My best advice for parents: ....

....

....

♡ Baby Shower ♡

Name: ....

Relationship to the parents / baby: ....

Wishes for the parents: ....

....

....

Wishes for the baby: ....

....

....

My best advice for parents: ....

....

....

♡ Baby Shower ♡

Name: ....

Relationship to the parents / baby: ....

Wishes for the parents: ....

....

....

Wishes for the baby: ....

....

....

My best advice for parents: ....

....

....

Baby Shower

Name: ....

Relationship to the parents / baby: ....

Wishes for the parents: ....

....

....

Wishes for the baby: ....

....

....

My best advice for parents: ....

....

....

Baby Shower

Name: ....

Relationship to the parents / baby: ....

Wishes for the parents: ....

....

....

Wishes for the baby: ....

....

....

My best advice for parents: ....

....

....

♡ Baby Shower ♡

Name: ....

Relationship to the parents / baby: ....

Wishes for the parents: ....

....

....

Wishes for the baby: ....

....

....

My best advice for parents: ....

....

....

Baby Shower

Name: ....

Relationship to the parents / baby: ....

Wishes for the parents: ....

....

....

Wishes for the baby: ....

....

....

My best advice for parents: ....

....

....

Baby Shower

Name: ....

Relationship to the parents / baby: ....

Wishes for the parents: ....

....

....

Wishes for the baby: ....

....

....

My best advice for parents: ....

....

....

Baby Shower

Name: ....

Relationship to the parents / baby: ....

Wishes for the parents: ....

....

....

Wishes for the baby: ....

....

....

My best advice for parents: ....

....

....

Baby Shower

Name: ....

Relationship to the parents / baby: ....

Wishes for the parents: ....

....

....

Wishes for the baby: ....

....

....

My best advice for parents: ....

....

....

Baby Shower

Name: ....

Relationship to the parents / baby: ....

Wishes for the parents: ....

....

....

Wishes for the baby: ....

....

....

My best advice for parents: ....

....

....

Baby Shower

Name: ....

Relationship to the parents / baby: ....

Wishes for the parents: ....

....

....

Wishes for the baby: ....

....

....

My best advice for parents: ....

....

....

♡ Baby Shower ♡

Name: ....

Relationship to the parents / baby: ....

Wishes for the parents: ....

....

....

Wishes for the baby: ....

....

....

My best advice for parents: ....

....

....

Baby Shower

Name: ....

Relationship to the parents / baby: ....

Wishes for the parents: ....

....

....

Wishes for the baby: ....

....

....

My best advice for parents: ....

....

....

♡ Baby Shower ♡

Name: ....

Relationship to the parents / baby: ....

Wishes for the parents: ....

....

....

Wishes for the baby: ....

....

....

My best advice for parents: ....

....

....

Baby Shower

Name: ....

Relationship to the parents / baby: ....

Wishes for the parents: ....

....

....

Wishes for the baby: ....

....

....

My best advice for parents: ....

....

....

Baby Shower

Name: ....

Relationship to the parents / baby: ....

Wishes for the parents: ....

....

....

Wishes for the baby: ....

....

....

My best advice for parents: ....

....

....

♡ Baby Shower ♡

Name: ....

Relationship to the parents / baby: ....

Wishes for the parents: ....

....

....

Wishes for the baby: ....

....

....

My best advice for parents: ....

....

....

Baby Shower

Name: ....

Relationship to the parents / baby: ....

Wishes for the parents: ....

....

....

Wishes for the baby: ....

....

....

My best advice for parents: ....

....

....

Baby Shower

Name: ....

Relationship to the parents / baby: ....

Wishes for the parents: ....

....

....

Wishes for the baby: ....

....

....

My best advice for parents: ....

....

....

Baby Shower

Name: ....

Relationship to the parents / baby: ....

Wishes for the parents: ....

....

....

Wishes for the baby: ....

....

....

My best advice for parents: ....

....

....

Baby Shower

Name: ....

Relationship to the parents / baby: ....

Wishes for the parents: ....

....

....

Wishes for the baby: ....

....

....

My best advice for parents: ....

....

....

Baby Shower

Name: ....

Relationship to the parents / baby: ....

Wishes for the parents: ....

....

....

Wishes for the baby: ....

....

....

My best advice for parents: ....

....

....

Baby Shower

Name: ....

Relationship to the parents / baby: ....

Wishes for the parents: ....

....

....

Wishes for the baby: ....

....

....

My best advice for parents: ....

....

....

Baby Shower

Name: ....

Relationship to the parents / baby: ....

Wishes for the parents: ....

....

....

Wishes for the baby: ....

....

....

My best advice for parents: ....

....

....

♡ Baby Shower ♡

Name: ....

Relationship to the parents / baby: ....

Wishes for the parents: ....

....

....

Wishes for the baby: ....

....

....

My best advice for parents: ....

....

....

Baby Shower

Name: ....

Relationship to the parents / baby: ....

Wishes for the parents: ....

....

....

Wishes for the baby: ....

....

....

My best advice for parents: ....

....

....

Baby Shower

Name: ....

Relationship to the parents / baby: ....

Wishes for the parents: ....

....

....

Wishes for the baby: ....

....

....

My best advice for parents: ....

....

....

Baby Shower

Name: ....

Relationship to the parents / baby: ....

Wishes for the parents: ....

....

....

Wishes for the baby: ....

....

....

My best advice for parents: ....

....

....

♡ Baby Shower ♡

Name: ....

Relationship to the parents / baby: ....

Wishes for the parents: ....

....

....

Wishes for the baby: ....

....

....

My best advice for parents: ....

....

....

Baby Shower

Name: ....

Relationship to the parents / baby: ....

Wishes for the parents: ....

....

....

Wishes for the baby: ....

....

....

My best advice for parents: ....

....

....

Baby Shower

Name: ....

Relationship to the parents / baby: ....

Wishes for the parents: ....

....

....

Wishes for the baby: ....

....

....

My best advice for parents: ....

....

....

Baby Shower

Name: ....

Relationship to the parents / baby: ....

Wishes for the parents: ....

....

....

Wishes for the baby: ....

....

....

My best advice for parents: ....

....

....

Baby Shower

Name: ....

Relationship to the parents / baby: ....

Wishes for the parents: ....

....

....

Wishes for the baby: ....

....

....

My best advice for parents: ....

....

....

♡ Baby Shower ♡

Name: ....

Relationship to the parents / baby: ....

Wishes for the parents: ....

....

....

Wishes for the baby: ....

....

....

My best advice for parents: ....

....

....

Baby Shower

Name: ....

Relationship to the parents / baby: ....

Wishes for the parents: ....

....

....

Wishes for the baby: ....

....

....

My best advice for parents: ....

....

....

♡ Baby Shower ♡

Name: ....

Relationship to the parents / baby: ....

Wishes for the parents: ....

....

....

Wishes for the baby: ....

....

....

My best advice for parents: ....

....

....

♡ Baby Shower ♡

Name: ....

Relationship to the parents / baby: ....

Wishes for the parents: ....

....

....

Wishes for the baby: ....

....

....

My best advice for parents: ....

....

....

Baby Shower

Name: ....

Relationship to the parents / baby: ....

Wishes for the parents: ....

....

....

Wishes for the baby: ....

....

....

My best advice for parents: ....

....

....

Baby Shower

Name: ....

Relationship to the parents / baby: ....

Wishes for the parents: ....

....

....

Wishes for the baby: ....

....

....

My best advice for parents: ....

....

....

Baby Shower

Name: ....

Relationship to the parents / baby: ....

Wishes for the parents: ....

....

....

Wishes for the baby: ....

....

....

My best advice for parents: ....

....

....

Baby Shower

Name: ....

Relationship to the parents / baby: ....

Wishes for the parents: ....

....

....

Wishes for the baby: ....

....

....

My best advice for parents: ....

....

....

Baby Shower

Name: ....

Relationship to the parents / baby: ....

Wishes for the parents: ....

....

....

Wishes for the baby: ....

....

....

My best advice for parents: ....

....

....

Baby Shower

Name: ....

Relationship to the parents / baby: ....

Wishes for the parents: ....

....

....

Wishes for the baby: ....

....

....

My best advice for parents: ....

....

....

Baby Shower

Name: ....

Relationship to the parents / baby: ....

Wishes for the parents: ....

....

....

Wishes for the baby: ....

....

....

My best advice for parents: ....

....

....

♡ Baby Shower ♡

Name: ....

Relationship to the parents / baby: ....

Wishes for the parents: ....

....

....

Wishes for the baby: ....

....

....

My best advice for parents: ....

....

....

♡ Baby Shower ♡

Name: ....

Relationship to the parents / baby: ....

Wishes for the parents: ....

....

....

Wishes for the baby: ....

....

....

My best advice for parents: ....

....

....

♡ Baby Shower ♡

Name: ....

Relationship to the parents / baby: ....

Wishes for the parents: ....

....

....

Wishes for the baby: ....

....

....

My best advice for parents: ....

....

....

♡ Baby Shower ♡

Name: ....

Relationship to the parents / baby: ....

Wishes for the parents: ....

....

....

Wishes for the baby: ....

....

....

My best advice for parents: ....

....

....

Baby Shower

Name: ....

Relationship to the parents / baby: ....

Wishes for the parents: ....

....

....

Wishes for the baby: ....

....

....

My best advice for parents: ....

....

....

♡ Baby Shower ♡

Name: ....

Relationship to the parents / baby: ....

Wishes for the parents: ....

....

....

Wishes for the baby: ....

....

....

My best advice for parents: ....

....

....

Baby Shower

Name: ....

Relationship to the parents / baby: ....

Wishes for the parents: ....

....

....

Wishes for the baby: ....

....

....

My best advice for parents: ....

....

....

Baby Shower

Name: ....

Relationship to the parents / baby: ....

Wishes for the parents: ....

....

....

Wishes for the baby: ....

....

....

My best advice for parents: ....

....

....

Baby Shower

Name: ....

Relationship to the parents / baby: ....

Wishes for the parents: ....

....

....

Wishes for the baby: ....

....

....

My best advice for parents: ....

....

....

Baby Shower

Name: ....

Relationship to the parents / baby: ....

Wishes for the parents: ....

....

....

Wishes for the baby: ....

....

....

My best advice for parents: ....

....

....

Baby Shower

Name: ....

Relationship to the parents / baby: ....

Wishes for the parents: ....

....

....

Wishes for the baby: ....

....

....

My best advice for parents: ....

....

....

Baby Shower

Name: ....

Relationship to the parents / baby: ....

Wishes for the parents: ....

....

....

Wishes for the baby: ....

....

....

My best advice for parents: ....

....

....

Baby Shower

Name: ....

Relationship to the parents / baby: ....

Wishes for the parents: ....

....

....

Wishes for the baby: ....

....

....

My best advice for parents: ....

....

....

♡ Baby Shower ♡

Name: ....

Relationship to the parents / baby: ....

Wishes for the parents: ....

....

....

Wishes for the baby: ....

....

....

My best advice for parents: ....

....

....

Printed in the USA
CPSIA information can be obtained
at www.ICGtesting.com
LVHW070155280823
756472LV00026B/1485